HOW TO SELECT DESIRED CONTRACT MANUFACTURER & GET 10X GROWTH

HOW TO SELECT DESIRED CONTRACT MANUFACTURER & GET 10X GROWTH

KESHAAV BHATIA

Worldwide Published by
Pendown Press

PENDOWN PRESS LLP

An ISO 9001 & ISO 14001 Certified Co.,

Regd. Office: 3767A, Kanhaiya Nagar,
Tri Nagar, Delhi-110035
Ph.: 8130886000, 9650072927
E-mail: info@pendownpress.com
Branch Office: 1A/2A, 20, Hari Sadan, Ansari Road,
Daryaganj, New Delhi-110002
Ph.: 011-45794768
Website: PendownPress.com

Edition: 2024
Price: ₹ 999/-
ISBN: 978-93-6338-888-8

Layout and Cover Designed by Pendown Graphics Team
Printed and Bound in India by Thomson Press India Ltd.

Table of Contents

SECTION 5

SECTION - 1

OUTSOURCING

Paving the Way for Growth: An Introduction

Outsourcing manufacturing today is a strategic move that many growth-conscious business owners are using to enhance their operational efficiency and competitive edge. If you are not doing so, you are missing out on one of the best and most effortless strategies to drive phenomenal growth.

By leveraging the expertise and resources of specialized manufacturing firms, you as a business can focus on your core competencies such as product design, marketing, and sales. This not only streamlines operations but also significantly reduces costs associated with labor, equipment, and facility management.

Scalability: The Top Benefit of Outsourcing

Outsourcing provides flexibility and scalability as you can adjust production levels based on market demand without the risks and costs associated with scaling internal operations up or down. It offers flexibility that allows businesses to adjust production levels according to market demand. Unlike scaling internal operations, which involves significant risks and costs, outsourcing enables companies to quickly increase or decrease production without financial and logistical burdens.

This adaptability is vital in today's fast-paced market environment, where consumer preferences can change rapidly. Being able to respond quickly to these shifts is necessary for maintaining a competitive edge.

For instance, if a new product becomes unexpectedly popular, outsourced operations can ramp up production to meet demand without the delays and expenses of hiring new staff or expanding facilities. Conversely, if demand decreases, companies can scale down operations just as easily, avoiding the costs of excess capacity.

This ability to respond dynamically to market conditions can be the difference between leveraging new opportunities and suffering from missed chances, ultimately determining a company's success or failure in a volatile marketplace.

This speedy response is crucial in today's fast-paced market environment, where consumer preferences can shift rapidly, and being able to respond quickly can be the difference between success and failure.

Allows Brands to Focus on Marketing with Greater Budgets & More Time on Their Hands

Outsourcing offers significant advantages by enabling brands to redirect their focus and resources towards marketing efforts. Here's how:

Cost Efficiency and Budget Allocation: When brands outsource specific functions, they often experience cost savings due to the reduced need for in-house staff, equipment, and other operational expenses. These savings create more financial room, allowing companies to allocate **larger budgets**

to their marketing initiatives. This increased funding can be used for various marketing activities such as advertising, digital campaigns, market research, and brand development.

Time Management, Resource Optimization & Strategic Focus - Outsourcing reduces the burden of daily operational tasks, which often consume a considerable amount of time and energy. By delegating these tasks to external experts, brands can free up their internal teams to focus on core activities that drive growth. With more time available, these teams can plan, strategize, and execute more comprehensive and effective marketing campaigns. With day-to-day operational responsibilities handled externally, brands can shift their strategic focus towards marketing.

Innovation and Creativity- Having more time and resources enables marketing teams to innovate and experiment with new ideas. They can explore creative approaches, test different marketing channels, and develop unique content that captures the audience's attention.

Improved Marketing Campaign Execution- With increased budgets and more focused efforts, brands can execute marketing campaigns more effectively. They can afford to invest in high-quality production, advanced marketing tools, and data analytics to measure and optimize campaign performance. This results in better reach, higher engagement, and **ultimately, greater return on investment (ROI) for marketing activities.**

In summary, by outsourcing certain operations, brands can achieve greater financial and time flexibility. This enables them to allocate more resources to marketing, focus on strategic growth, and enhance the creativity and effectiveness of their campaigns. With outsourcing, your operation costs remain fixed and you also become free from day-to-day firefighting operations, this allows you to free up resources for bigger & better Marketing Budgets and effective strategizing & execution.

Brands Become CAPEX & OPEX Light by Outsourcing

Outsourcing allows brands to significantly reduce both capital expenditures (CAPEX) and operational expenditures (OPEX).

By partnering with external service providers, companies no longer need to invest heavily in infrastructure, equipment, or long-term assets required for in-house operations, thereby becoming **CAPEX-light.**

Additionally, outsourcing **minimizes OPEX** by lowering the costs associated with hiring, training, and maintaining a large workforce, as well as expenses related to utilities, maintenance, and administrative overhead.

This efficiency translates into more available resources that can be redirected toward marketing and brand-building activities by enhancing brand visibility and engaging with consumers more effectively. Investments in marketing initiatives such as digital campaigns, social media outreach, content creation, and market research can drive brand growth and customer loyalty.

Outsourcing Manufacturing Allows Penetration into Untapped Markets More Effectively

Outsourcing manufacturing to different regions around the country/world can significantly enhance a company's ability to tap into new markets. By partnering with manufacturers located in key regions (especially those far away from your current production facility), businesses can strategically position themselves to better serve local markets.

Reduced Shipping Costs and Minimizing Tariffs: Manufacturing products closer to the target markets can drastically reduce shipping costs and delivery times. This not only cuts down on expenses but also improves customer satisfaction by enabling faster product availability.

Enhanced Local Market Service: Having a manufacturing presence in various regions allows companies to cater to the specific needs and preferences of local consumers. This proximity to customers can lead to better market responsiveness and quicker adjustments to products based on local demand.

Insights into Market Trends and Customer Needs: Outsourcing to different regions gives businesses a direct understanding to diverse market trends and customer behaviors. Local manufacturing partners can provide valuable insights into emerging trends, consumer preferences, and potential demand shifts.

Fostering Innovation and Growth- This real-time information gained from regional outsourcing partners fosters innovation, enabling companies to develop products that resonate with local markets and stay ahead of competitors. **Access to various regional insights and customer feedback can inspire new ideas and drive innovation.** Companies can leverage these insights to improve existing products, develop new offerings, and tailor marketing strategies to better align with regional expectations. This continuous feedback loop between local markets and global operations promotes sustained growth and market relevance.

Enables Cost Reduction

One of the primary benefits of outsourcing manufacturing is cost reduction. You can avoid the high costs of setting up and maintaining manufacturing facilities, purchasing machinery, and hiring and training workers. Instead, you can benefit from the economies of scale that these established manufacturing partners offer. These savings can then be reinvested into other areas of your business, such as research and development, enhancing product offerings, and expanding market reach.

Access to Advanced Technology and Skilled Labor

Manufacturing partners often have the latest equipment and a workforce trained in the most up-to-date techniques. This can lead to higher quality products, improved production efficiency, and reduced time-to-market. For small and medium-sized enterprises, in particular, outsourcing levels the playing field, allowing them to compete with larger companies without the need for substantial capital investment.

As the Indian FMCG Food Sector experiences rapid growth, driven by rising disposable incomes, rapid urbanization, and changing consumer preferences, **outsourcing manufacturing has become a lifesaver and is no longer just an option but your go-to move if you want to thrive & not just survive. Partnering with an outsourcing manufacturing expert can make the difference between being average and being phenomenally profitable.**

In summary, outsourcing manufacturing offers numerous benefits for business owners, including cost savings, access to advanced technology and skilled labor, operational flexibility, and the ability to compete on a global scale. By focusing on their core competencies and leveraging the strengths of specialized manufacturing partners, businesses can drive innovation, improve product quality, and ultimately boost profitability, making outsourcing a compelling strategy for modern enterprises.

I am sharing below a Case Study that will demonstrate the transformational power and benefits of outsourcing as a high-growth strategic partnership.

A Brand is Empowered by Outsourcing to Grow from 150 Cr to 550 Cr in less than 5 Years!

The Client: A Leading Player in the FMCG Food Sector-Candy Vertical

The Challenges: The brand was facing 7 major challenges in diverse areas of operations and was unable to scale up.

1. **Untapped Markets due to lack of production and storage facilities in certain areas.**

   The Solution: West Bengal and the North East were the major untapped markets until the client partnered with us in 2015. Once we came on board as Growth Partners and production commenced at our local facilities, an additional 30,000 cartons per month (equivalent to 4,000 tons or 1 billion candies per year) began to penetrate these markets, making 1 billion children, adults, and consumers happy.

The Phenomenal Result: Thus, we helped the brand expand and penetrate untapped markets leading to a request to double our production capacities.

2. **Cost of High Inventory to cater promptly to high-demand areas.**

   The Solution: Being strategically located at the Chicken Neck of India allowed us to efficiently cater to nearby markets. Had the client not partnered with us and used our plant they would have incurred huge inventory as well as capital costs.

   The Phenomenal Result: By maintaining higher inventories, we ensured low capital investment for the brand since everything produced was sold promptly, keeping investment levels minimal.

3. **High Overheads leading to Higher Operational Costs**

   The Solution: Brands often have extensive upper management with high salary packages. However, partnering with us eliminated the need for a heavy upper management team as all the processes were delegated to us.

   The Phenomenal Result: By outsourcing work to us, they managed to keep operation costs lean & low, allowing them to serve the market better in terms of price and leverage this edge.

4. **Constant Fire-Fighting Due to the Headaches of Operations**

   The Solution: Managing operations can lead to significant headaches and loss of peace of mind, particularly due to the complexities and challenges involved. By outsourcing to us, the brand alleviated these burdens, allowing them to focus on their core activities.

   The Phenomenal Result: This not only enhanced efficiency but also ensured better market performance without the constant stress of operational issues.

5. **High Wastages of RM & PM up to 5-7 %**

   The Solution: Partnering with us meant having access to our experience & expertise in the field. With time, study, and knowledge, we helped the brand reduce the wastage of a new product line from 5-7% to 2% within a stipulated period.

   The Phenomenal Result: This reduction in wastage contributed to a significant rise in profits.

6. **More CAPEX**

   The Solution: Partnering with us meant that the brand did not have to invest heavily in a world-class manufacturing facility to keep up with the market demand. We provided them with a ready state-of-the-art production facility.

   The Phenomenal Result: What the brand freed up in Capital Expenditure (CAPEX) it invested into Brand Building to establish itself in the minds of its customers.

7. **Longer Lead Times in the Supply Chain**

   The Solution: Thanks to our strategic location, we could efficiently serve nearby markets in Bengal, Assam, Sikkim, and all seven northeastern states promptly. This would have been impossible without our plant

   The Phenomenal Result: The supply that earlier used to take 10-12 days to reach these markets could now be supplied within a day.

8. **The Overall Impact on Growth**

   The cumulative effect of overcoming all the 7 challenges blocking growth by outsourcing and partnering with a growth partner was that the brand leapt from 150 Cr to 550 Cr in under 5 years. Isn't that transformational?

In the coming chapters of the book, I will delve and share with you in detail the burning challenges of the FMCG Food Industry, the need for an outsourcing growth partner, and the growth sutras. Additionally, I will also bust some myths that keep you from onboarding a growth partner and keep your growth hostage. And yes, I will also show you what to look for in a growth partner to choose the perfect fit!

Your Growth Partner

Keshaav Bhatia

SECTION - 2

OUTSOURCING

Who Am I & What Do I Do?

Hello & welcome to the first step of standing out from your competition.

With all the promises I've made in the chapter above, I'm sure you must be curious to know who is this man and how is he so confident about sharing this business-transforming knowledge.

My name is Keshaav Bhatia & I am a Third-Party Manufacturing Expert.

I am the Managing Director of Gobind Ram Kahan Chand an MSME that is firmly established as a quality third-party manufacturer in the FMCG food sector.

As I reflect on the journey of GRKC, I am filled with immense pride and a profound sense of responsibility. Our heritage is not just a testament to our longevity but a story of continuous evolution, resilience, and commitment to excellence. Allow me to take you through the legacy and achievements of GRKC, and you will understand why I can discuss outsourcing as a strategic imperative for FMCG food companies so thoroughly and confidently. As a 6th generation entrepreneur in this area, I have gathered vast learnings, experience and expertise.

The Heritage and Legacy of GRKC

GRKC is a 200-year-old organization, deeply rooted in the marketing and manufacturing of spices, confectionery, biscuits, and Ayurvedic natural supplements. Our journey began in Lahore, during the era when the city was a bustling hub of commerce and culture.

Documented by historian Pran Neville in his book, Lahore — A Sentimental Journey, as the most renowned sharbat makers of the city, our origins trace back to a time when our forefathers laid the foundation of what would become a legacy of quality and innovation.

Even today we have maintained that stamp of quality and commitment to deliver only the best in both products and processes.

Gobind Ram Kahan Chand was a well-known sharbat maker with a main shop in Kesera Bazaar and branches in Anarkali & Nisbet Road. They were famous for preparing murabbas of mangoes and other fruits and distilling them from various herbs.

- Pran Nevile in Lahore: A Sentimental Journey

In the early days, GRKC was involved in producing a variety of products that catered to the local market's demands. Our initial focus was on creating syrups, jams, and Ayurvedic herbal products, which quickly gained popularity due to their exceptional quality and effectiveness. This success set the stage for future growth and diversification.

After the partition, our family relocated to Delhi, bringing with us a rich legacy and an unwavering commitment to excellence. The second leg of our journey began with a modest plant in Delhi, manufacturing syrups, jams, and Ayurveda herbal products. Over time, we diversified our portfolio to include biscuits, spices, and confectionery, continually expanding our capacities and capabilities.

Today, we proudly operate multiple state-of-the-art plants:

- Our first plant in Delhi, dedicated to syrups, jams, and Ayurveda herbal products.
- Our second plant, which diversified into biscuits with a monthly capacity of 3000 MT and spices with a monthly capacity of 1000 MT.
- Our fourth plant, specializing in confectionery with a monthly capacity of 600 MT.

- Additional plants dedicated to biscuits and spices, further enhancing our production capabilities.

This extensive infrastructure allows us to process approximately 60,000 tons of food products annually. We have manufactured and processed over 120,000 tons of spices, 28,000 tons of confectionery, and 500,000 tons of biscuits to date.

This track record not only highlights our capacity but also our unwavering commitment to quality and innovation.

Business Ethics & Delivery

At GRKC, we embrace the concept of clean labels, ensuring that our products are free from artificial ingredients. This philosophy aligns with our belief in food as medicine, promoting health and well-being through natural and wholesome ingredients.

Our dedication to this principle has established us as a trusted and reliable supplier, serving numerous large organizations for over three decades.

Our commitment to on-time delivery has significantly increased material sales for our clients, demonstrating our reliability and efficiency.

This meticulous attention to detail ensures that our products meet the highest standards of quality and safety.

Why Am I So Confident in Discussing Outsourcing?

My experience and tenure at GRKC have provided me with a deep understanding of the FMCG sector and the intricacies of outsourcing. I have witnessed firsthand the transformative impact of strategic outsourcing on businesses, allowing them to scale up, tap into new markets, and achieve operational excellence without the burden of extensive capital investments.

Throughout my career, I have had the privilege of working closely with numerous brands, helping them navigate the complexities of production, logistics, and market expansion. Our 'One Product for One Client' principle has fostered trust and exclusivity, ensuring that each client's unique needs are met with precision and care.

Our professional approach, characterized by strict adherence to SOPs, rigorous audits, and confidentiality agreements, has consistently delivered outstanding results. Transparency is at the core of our operations, with daily reports on production progress, quality assessments, and CRM updates, ensuring that our clients are always informed and in control.

Our core philosophy & policy of "One Product for One Client Only" ensures exclusivity and trust for our clients.

Our ability to adapt to changing market dynamics and client needs, coupled with our robust infrastructure and compliance with industry standards, positions us as a partner of choice for any FMCG food company looking to outsource.

In conclusion, the heritage, legacy, and achievements of GRKC underscore our expertise and reliability in the FMCG sector. My journey with GRKC has equipped me with the insights and experience to advocate for outsourcing as a strategic approach to achieving growth and operational efficiency.

By choosing the right Growth Partner, you can unlock your full potential and navigate the challenges of the ever-evolving market landscape with confidence and ease.

So, stay excited and stay with me as I share in detail all that I promised in chapter 1.........

SECTION - 3

OUTSOURCING

The 7 Burning Challenges of Every Business Owner in the FMCG Food Sector

The fast-moving consumer goods (FMCG) food sector in India is a dynamic and rapidly evolving industry, characterized by fierce competition and ever-changing consumer preferences. For brands to thrive, they must navigate multiple challenges that can impede growth and profitability. These challenges range from logistical constraints and high operational costs to managing extensive inventories and ensuring quick turnaround times in the supply chain.

Having worked closely with FMCG business owners in the food sector for decades, I have observed, understood and solved their challenges for nearly two decades. While the nature of business varies from business to business, I have identified that there are 7 challenges that are universal to all FMCG businesses in this sector. One effective solution that has emerged is the strategic outsourcing of manufacturing operations.

Here I am sharing these universal pain points and how to overcome these with strategic outsourcing with an expert growth partner.

This approach not only addresses these challenges head-on but also enables brands to focus on their core competencies, drive innovation, and expand their market reach. The following case studies illustrate how outsourcing has helped FMCG brands overcome critical obstacles and achieve remarkable success.

Challenge 1: Logistics - Tapping Untapped Markets

A major challenge for any business owner is managing logistics, Most FMCG business owners remain stuck and are unable to scale up and tap new markets as they cannot afford to have manufacturing facilities pan-India, as this would involve huge investments and pose operational hazards. In such a scenario, your business stays limited in its growth, whereas an out-of-the-box approach could help you fulfill your potential and your dreams.

Having a strategic growth partner in areas where you do not have your own manufacturing or storage facilities can resolve this challenge in a jiffy.

For Example, A mid-sized confectionery brand struggled to access the markets of southern India due to logistical complexities. By partnering with a strategically located manufacturing facility in the region, the brand began production and penetrated these regions with great intensity and ready reach. This satisfied a vast number of consumers and helped the brand scale up and expand smoothly without any strain on its existing human & physical resources & infrastructure.

Challenge 2: Managing Inventory

Managing inventory efficiently is another critical challenge for FMCG businesses. Extensive inventories can tie up significant capital, which could otherwise be used for growth and innovation. Finding a balance between having enough stock to meet demand and not overstocking is crucial.

Take the case of a leading Flour brand that faced inventory management challenges until it partnered with a manufacturing facility strategically located in the region of highest demand. This location allowed the company to supply higher inventories and ensure low capital investment, as everything produced was promptly sold. Without this plant, the company would have incurred significant capital costs to maintain large stocks. This case illustrates the importance of strategic location and efficient inventory management in reducing costs and improving cash flow.

Challenge 3: Reducing High Overheads and Operational Costs

High overheads and operational costs are common hurdles for FMCG companies. Extensive management structures and high salary packages can drain resources that could be better used elsewhere.

This is evident from the case of a prominent snack brand with a large upper management structure that faced elevated operational costs. By outsourcing manufacturing to a specialized facility, the brand managed to reduce these costs significantly. For instance, the brand cut its operational expenses by 25% after the partnership, allowing it to offer competitive pricing and improve market share without compromising on quality. This reduction in overheads helped the company allocate more resources to product development and marketing.

Challenge 4: Alleviating Operational Headaches

Managing day-to-day operations can be a significant headache, diverting attention from core business activities and strategic growth initiatives.

An Ayurvedic products company experienced operational inefficiencies that affected its market performance. By outsourcing to a manufacturing partner, the company alleviated these burdens, allowing its leadership team to focus on core activities like marketing and product development. This strategic shift not only enhanced efficiency but also ensured better market performance without the constant stress of operational issues.

Challenge 5: Reducing Wastages of Raw and Packaging Materials

Wastage of raw materials (RM) and packaging materials (PM) can severely impact profitability. Efficient waste management is crucial for maintaining margins. Partnering with growth partners who have the requisite expertise and R&D mindsets as well as capabilities can often lead you to find new ways of addressing and solving the challenges.

As demonstrated by a bakery sector company that faced wastages of up to 5-7% for a new product line. However, through diligent study and knowledge application, the manufacturing partner helped reduce this wastage to 2% within a stipulated period. This reduction translated to substantial cost savings and a significant rise in profits, underscoring the importance of continuous improvement and efficiency in manufacturing processes.

Challenge 6: Minimizing Capital Expenditure (CAPEX)

Minimizing capital expenditure while maintaining efficiency is essential for FMCG brands. Outsourcing can help achieve this balance by reducing the need for large upfront investments in manufacturing infrastructure.

A leading FMCG brand that operated with minimal capital expenditure and lean operating expenses by outsourcing its manufacturing showcases this principle perfectly. For instance, a biscuit brand saved 100% on Capex by outsourcing production, allowing it to allocate more resources to marketing and innovation. This strategic allocation of resources has been instrumental in driving the brand's growth and market penetration.

Challenge 7: Reducing Lead Times in the Supply Chain

In the FMCG Food Sector, long lead times in the supply chain can hinder market performance. Quick turnaround is essential for maintaining product freshness and meeting consumer demand. This proves to be quite a challenge in this sector.

Example: A confectionery brand based in the north-eastern region of India faced significant delays in serving markets in the western region. Without a local plant, it would take 10-12 days for supplies to reach these markets. However, by partnering with a strategically located manufacturing facility, the brand was able to supply materials within a day. This drastic reduction in lead times was critical for maintaining product freshness and meeting consumer demand promptly.

As a result, the brand saw a 50% increase in sales in these regions, highlighting the importance of efficient supply chain management.

In conclusion, the FMCG food sector faces numerous challenges that can hinder growth and profitability. However, strategic outsourcing of manufacturing operations offers a viable solution, enabling brands to overcome these obstacles, optimize costs, and achieve sustainable success. Through real-world examples and case studies, the transformative impact of outsourcing on logistics, inventory management, operational costs, and overall effectivity, efficiency and need for a growth partner is clearly demonstrated.

SECTION - 4

OUTSOURCING

The 7 Growth Sutras: Outsourcing Needs Not Just a Partner but the Right Partner

In the competitive and dynamic FMCG food sector, finding the right outsourcing partner can be the difference between merely surviving and thriving. Here are seven critical factors that demonstrate why choosing the right partner is essential for success.

1. **Is Your Growth Partner a Trustworthy Manufacturer for Big Brands with Exclusivity?**

   A cornerstone of success lies in trust, especially when it comes to handling big brands. A reliable manufacturing partner understands the importance of exclusivity. Operating on the principle of 'One Product for One Client,' they dedicate production and packaging lines exclusively to each client. This not only fosters trust but also ensures that unique recipes and product integrity are maintained, ensuring optimal demand fulfillment and giving brands a competitive edge in the market.

   For Example, a large candy manufacturer sought a partner who could offer exclusive production lines. By collaborating with a manufacturer committed to producing only their products on designated lines, the brand ensured that their unique recipes and production techniques remained confidential. This strategic move not only facilitated the confidentiality of their renowned recipes but also helped in swiftly meeting regional demands.

The resultant trust allowed them to be mentally free to introduce new product lines with confidence, significantly boosting their market share. Imagine a leading confectionery brand seeking to expand into new regions., thereby solidifying their market position.

2. Does Your Growth Partner Have a Professional Approach?

Professionalism is the bedrock of any successful partnership. Ensure that your outsourcing partner has a system-based approach right from:

- Maintaining the confidentiality of recipes, raw materials & bill of materials (BOM) and adhering to standard operating procedures (SOPs).
- Checklists to ensure compliance with regulations & processes.
- A Finacle-based workflow system
- A Production Management System (PMS) focusing on production planning & control.
- A proper Inventory Management System.
- A proper Quality Control (QC) system is in place.
- An accurate & efficient Management Information System (MIS).

This systematic & disciplined approach not only ensures efficiency in operations & consistency in quality but also instills confidence & trust in clients, guaranteeing reliable and superior outcomes.

This is well illustrated by an FMCG company that needed a partner for its Sherbet line who could maintain strict confidentiality and adhere to detailed SOPs. The chosen partner's professional approach, which included regular audits and strict process controls, resulted in the successful launch of a new health drink. The product quickly gained market acceptance due to its consistent quality and taste, reflecting the partner's professional handling.

3. Can Your Growth Partner Work on Your Terms & Controlled Pricing?

Transparency and efficiency form the backbone of cost-effective production and are key to maintaining controlled pricing. A proficient outsourcing partner provides real-time insights through comprehensive daily reports on production progress, packaging updates, quality assessments, and customer relationship management (CRM). An efficient partner ensures that minimal resources yield maximum output; by optimizing resource utilization and maintaining high productivity levels, they ensure competitive pricing without compromising on quality.

This is clearly evidenced in the example of a snack food company which partnered with a manufacturer that provided daily reports on production efficiency, packaging quality, and CRM activities. This transparency allowed the company to monitor and adjust processes in real-time, ensuring consistent product quality and timely delivery. Daily reports on production metrics and quality benchmarks allowed the brand to fine-tune operations swiftly, achieving optimal cost-effectiveness. As a result, the brand maintained competitive pricing, enhancing its market position.

4. **Does Your Growth Partner Ensure Delivery On-Time Every Time?**

   Timely delivery is non-negotiable in meeting market demands and maximizing profitability, it is crucial for increasing market reach and boosting sales and profits. An esteemed outsourcing partner prioritizes punctuality, ensuring products reach shelves promptly, delivering on time, every time, leading to satisfied customers and repeat business.

   This commitment not only boosts customer satisfaction but also enhances sales figures, driving sustained growth and profitability for brands.

   This is well showcased by a flour brand that was experiencing frequent delays in product delivery, affecting its market reach. After partnering with a reliable manufacturer who prioritized on-time delivery, the company's distribution network became more efficient. Sales increased by 20% within six months, demonstrating the impact of timely delivery on market expansion and profitability.

5. **Is Your Growth Partner Committed to the Highest Standard of Delivery?**

   Exceeding customer expectations hinges on maintaining the highest standards throughout the production and delivery process. A top-tier outsourcing partner excels in meticulous planning, seamless logistics, and stringent quality control measures. Each stage—from order processing to final delivery—is meticulously executed to ensure superior product quality and reliability, thereby cultivating trust and long-term loyalty. This commitment ensures that every stage of the process, from order processing to final delivery, exceeds customer expectations.

For instance, look at this bakery brand that was struggling with quality issues with a partner, and decided to look for a quality-conscious partner. After much thought and deliberation, they partnered with a manufacturer known for its high standards of delivery. The manufacturer's meticulous planning and rigorous quality checks ensured that every batch of products met the brand's high standards. Customer feedback improved, and the brand's reputation for quality grew, resulting in increased market share. This unwavering commitment to excellence not only enhanced the brand's reputation but also fortified its position as a market leader in premium baked goods.

6. **Is Your Growth Partner Adaptable: Can They Calibrate to Your Changing Needs & Desires?**

Adaptability is key to navigating the evolving landscape of consumer preferences and market dynamics. A forward-thinking outsourcing partner embraces an adaptive mindset, swiftly adjusting operations to align with client's evolving needs and desires. This flexibility ensures continual innovation and the ability to surpass expectations, fostering enduring satisfaction and loyalty in collaborative ventures through being dynamic and responsive.

This quality was perfectly embodied by a candy brand's growth partner. This brand frequently introduced new flavors to keep up with market trends. Their manufacturing partner's adaptive mindset and flexible operations allowed for quick adjustments in production lines. This agility enabled the company to launch new products faster than competitors, keeping them at the forefront of the market.

7. **Does Your Growth Partner Have a History of Compliance with Ready Infrastructure?**

   Compliance with industry standards and regulatory requirements is non-negotiable in safeguarding brand reputation and ensuring product safety. A reputable outsourcing partner boasts a proven track record of 100% compliance with client-specific SOPs and regulatory frameworks. A manufacturer's ability to ensure 100% compliance with client SOPs and regulatory standards, such as FSSAI regulations, is crucial. A robust infrastructure setup enables seamless adherence to these standards, ensuring quality and safety throughout production.

   For example, a canned food brand required strict compliance with FSSAI regulations. By partnering with a manufacturer with a proven track record of compliance and a well-established infrastructure, the brand ensured that all products met regulatory standards. This compliance not only safeguarded the brand's reputation but also facilitated smooth market entry for new products.

   In conclusion, outsourcing manufacturing in the FMCG food sector necessitates not just any partner but the right partner. By focusing on exclusivity, professionalism, transparency, timely delivery, high standards, adaptability, and compliance, brands can overcome challenges and achieve sustainable growth and success.

SECTION - 5

OUTSOURCING

Establishing Criteria for Selecting a Reliable Vendor

When entering a partnership with an outsourcing manufacturer, to ensure that your outsourcing partner proves to be your growth partner it is essential to know the criteria for selecting the right vendor.

Zeroing in on the right partner will ensure the success and consistency of your operations.

Drawing from my extensive experience, I have emphasized certain key elements below that will ensure that you choose a reliable and profitable outsourcing partner.

Central to your selection criteria is a requirement for the outsourcing partner to have a systematic approach within their internal operations. This approach is anchored in the rigorous measurement and reporting of critical aspects, ensuring transparency and reliability throughout the partnership.

1. System-Based Approach

Central to your selection criteria is a requirement for the outsourcing partner to have a systematic approach within their internal operations. This approach is anchored in the rigorous measurement and reporting of critical aspects, ensuring transparency and reliability throughout the partnership. Here's what to look for.

- **Checklist-Based MIS Reports:** Choose a partner who can provide you with timely and consistent Management Information System (MIS) reports that are structured around comprehensive checklists. These reports serve as a means for tracking adherence to quality standards and operational protocols. These reports keep you in the loop and thus help establish trust and confidence in the relationship.

Cleaning
CHECKLIST

DATE: ____________

№	ACTIVITIES	✓
1	Dust all surfaces including shelves, furniture	
2	Clean mirrors and glass surfaces using a glass cleaner	
3	Vacuum carpets and area rugs	
4	Sweep and mop hard floors	
5	Clean and disinfect toilets, sinks, and showers	
6	Scrub and disinfect kitchen countertops and sinks	
7	Clean the kitchen appliances such as the stove, oven, fridge	
8	Wipe down cabinets and drawers in the kitchen, bathroom	
9	Clean and disinfect light switches, doorknobs	
10	Wash and change bed linens	
11	Dust blinds and window sills	
12	Clean windows inside and out	
13	Clean and disinfect garbage cans	
14	Vacuum furniture and upholstery	
15	Clean and disinfect pet areas	
16	Wipe down baseboards and molding	
17	Dust ceiling fans and light fixtures	
18	Clean and disinfect computer keyboards and screens	
19	Organize and declutter living spaces	
20	Sweep and tidy outdoor areas such as porches and patios	

- **Flow Management System:** The partner you choose must have an efficient flow management system. This is essential for optimizing processes and minimizing inefficiencies. It ensures smooth coordination across different stages of production and supply chain management.

The Flowchart

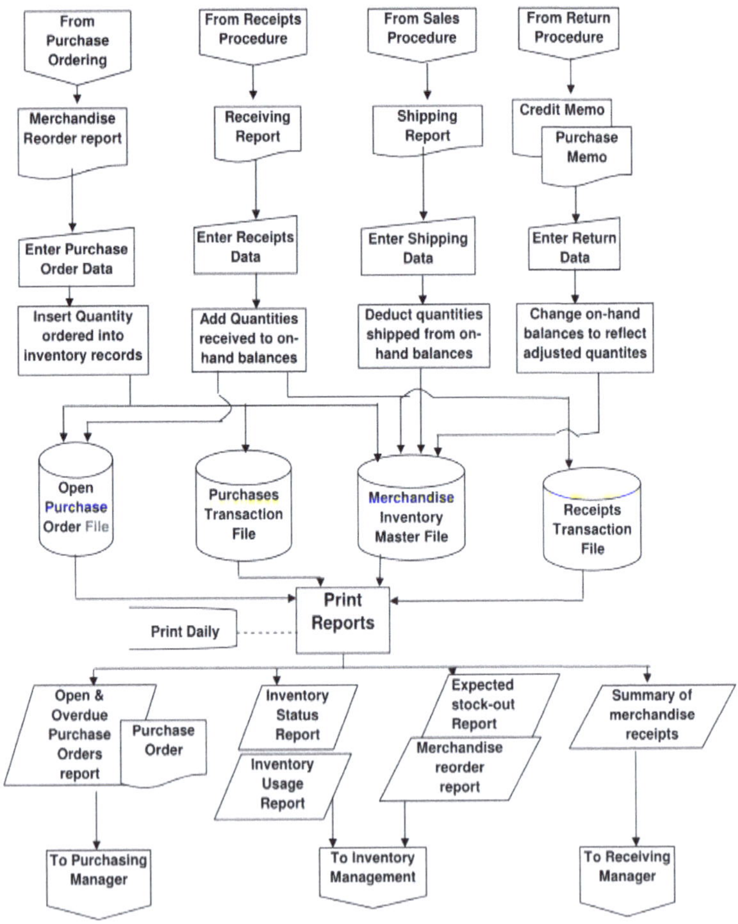

- **Inventory Management System:** Effective management of inventory is critical for maintaining supply chain continuity and meeting production demands when they vary due to market fluctuations without overstocking or shortages. Choose a partner who is capable of optimum inventory management.

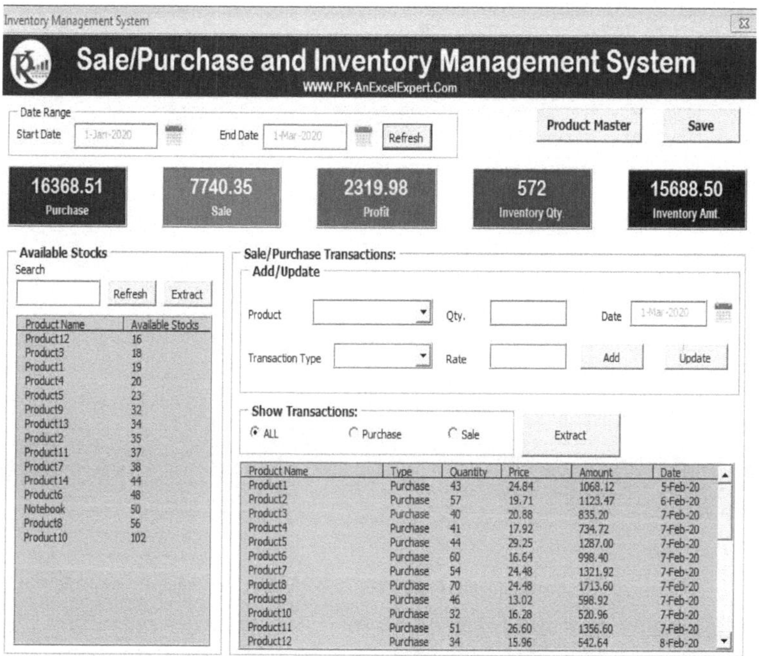

- **Production Management System (PPC):** The partner you choose should demonstrate proficiency in Production Planning and Control (PPC), which plays an important role in scheduling production activities, optimizing resource utilization, and meeting delivery deadlines.

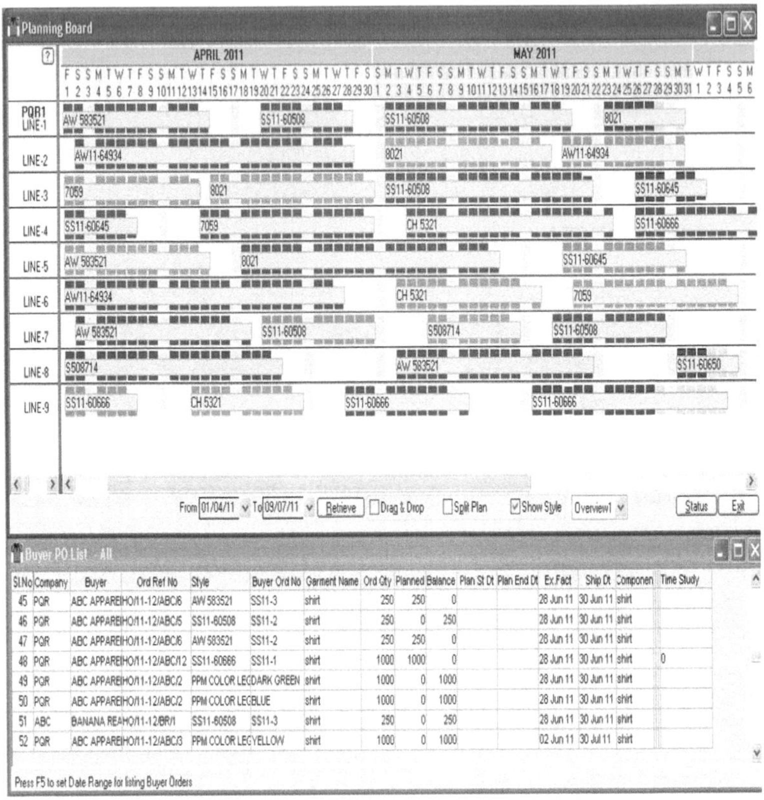

- **Quality Management System (QMS):** A vigilant & rigorous Quality Management System (QMS) is non-negotiable in ensuring consistent product quality. It means your partner should have systematic processes for quality assurance, control, and improvement throughout all stages of production.

ISO 9001 Audit Example Report

Audit — 3 flagged, 93.33%

Context of the Organization

100%

Have all external and internal issues that are relevant to your organization's purpose and the achievement of customer satisfaction and the organization's strategic direction been determined?	Yes
Are these issues reviewed and monitored on a regular basis?	Yes
Have the needs and expectations of interested parties that are relevant to the QMS been determined?	Yes
Was the scope of your QMS determined whilst taking into account all the external and internal issues, the needs of interested parties and the scope your products and services?	Yes
Is your QMS established, and does it include a description of the processes required and their sequence and interaction?	Yes
Have the criteria for managing these processes and their interaction been established?	Yes
Have all responsibilities, methods, measurements and related performance indicators, needed to ensure the effective operation and control, been established?	Yes

Leadership

2 flagged, 71.4%

Has top management taken accountability for the effectiveness of the QMS?	Yes
Have the policy and objectives for the QMS, which are compatible with the strategic direction of the organization, been established and communicated?	No
There are managers who can't confirm knowledge of the QMS	
Have the objectives been established at relevant departmental and individual levels with the business?	No
There are department heads who are currently unaware of the objectives.	
Have the requirements for the QMS been integrated into the business processes and have management promoted awareness of the process approach?	Yes
Awareness was promoted but it appears it is not enough because of the unaware individuals.	
Have customer requirements and applicable statutory and regulatory requirements been determined, met and	Yes

SafetyCulture

2. Data-Driven Decision Making

The presence of all the structured systems listed above lays the foundation for meaningful daily reports, audits, quality check parameters, proficiency assessments, and efficiency evaluations. All these measures are not merely procedural. Instead, **they are essential for data-driven decision-making to enable, cost-inventory optimization & enhance profitability.:**

- **Data Comparison:** Historical data and benchmarks allow for informed decision-making and continuous improvement initiatives. Data comparison plays a crucial role in making informed decisions and driving continuous improvement.

  By analyzing historical data and benchmarks, you can gain valuable insights into your performance over time. This comparison will allow you to identify trends, strengths, and areas that need improvement.

  For instance, if production efficiency has increased over the past year, the data from all these reports can highlight the successful strategies that have made this improvement possible. On the other hand, if there are recurring issues, the data can pinpoint where processes may be falling short.

  Benchmarking against industry standards or competitors also provides a clear picture of where you as a brand stand in the market. This comprehensive understanding will enable you to make strategic decisions that are based on evidence rather than just random assumptions. Additionally, continuous monitoring and comparison of data brings about a culture of ongoing improvement, encouraging teams to refine processes, adopt best practices, and innovate to stay ahead.

- **Root Cause Analysis:** When deviations occur, a data-driven approach facilitates quick identification of root causes, enabling timely corrective actions. By using a data-driven approach, you can quickly identify the underlying causes of any deviations or problems. Instead of guessing or making assumptions.

  For example, if a production line is experiencing delays, data can reveal whether the problem lies in equipment malfunctions, supply chain disruptions, or workforce inefficiencies. Once the root cause is identified, timely corrective actions can be implemented to resolve the issue. This might involve repairing or replacing faulty equipment, adjusting supply chain processes, or providing additional training to employees. The goal is to fix the problem at its source to prevent it from recurring. This proactive and systematic approach ensures that issues are not just temporarily patched up but are resolved in a way that enhances overall efficiency and reliability.

  If your partner is thorough with their systems and reports, they will be able to make all these decisions quickly while keeping you updated and informed as well. **This not only sets high standards of efficiency and delivery but also brings trust and transparency to the relationship.**

3. Ensuring 100% Satisfaction and Trust

Ultimately, the implementation of these criteria is geared towards achieving 100% satisfaction and trust in your relationship with your contract manufacturing outsourcing partner.

By adhering to systematic processes and leveraging data for insights, manufacturers can consistently meet and exceed expectations.

- **Customer-Centric Focus:** A customer-centric focus means that manufacturers design their operations to closely align with the needs and expectations of their customers. This approach ensures that the manufacturer is not only aware of what customers want but is also agile enough to adapt to changing demands quickly.

  For instance, if a manufacturer understands that customers prefer faster delivery times or have specific quality standards, they will adjust their production processes, inventory management, and supply chain logistics to meet those preferences. This might involve implementing more flexible production schedules, optimizing distribution channels, or enhancing quality control measures.

  By staying in tune with customer feedback and market trends, manufacturers can rapidly adjust their operations to address emerging needs or preferences. This responsiveness helps them remain competitive and relevant, building stronger customer relationships and ensuring high levels of satisfaction. You need to choose a partner who has the mindset & technical & human-resource capability to respond to the changes & tweaks you need as per customer feedback.

  A flexible & responsive growth partner will support & enable you to be more proactive rather than reactive, continuously refining their processes and offerings to better serve their customers and adapt to an ever-changing market landscape.

- **Continuous Improvement:** Commitment to ongoing improvement drives innovation and operational excellence, establishing your outsourcing partner as a proactive partner in mutual success.

Continuous improvement is about finding ways to do things better. When your partner is committed to ongoing improvement, they are constantly looking for ways to enhance their processes, products, and services. This dedication to getting better leads to innovation, where new ideas and solutions are developed to stay ahead of the competition.

For example, a manufacturer might regularly review their production methods to identify areas where they can be more efficient or reduce waste. They might invest in new technology, train their staff, or refine their procedures to boost quality and speed. This ongoing effort not only improves their own operations but also benefits their partners by ensuring they receive better products and services.

This approach helps them meet changing demands, solve problems before they escalate, and maintain high standards. Ultimately, it builds a strong foundation for long-term success and a positive, collaborative relationship with their partners.

In conclusion, the selection of a contract manufacturer is a strategic decision that transcends mere capability; it hinges on the systematic integration of processes and a steadfast commitment to quality and transparency. **By upholding these criteria, you will easily be able to identify and work with the right outsourcing partner who will prove to be your partner**

in phenomenal growth, not only delivering results but also driving continuous growth and innovation.

As I conclude this sharing of insights into the transformative benefits of outsourcing manufacturing, I am sure that it must be clear to you, that this strategic approach is not just a trend but a crucial move for businesses aiming to thrive in today's competitive landscape.

Outsourcing offers unparalleled advantages, from enhancing scalability and reducing costs to freeing up resources for strategic marketing and innovation. By partnering with specialized manufacturing firms, companies can focus on what they do best—designing, marketing, and growing their brand—while leaving the complexities of production to their expert outsourcing partners.

The various real-world examples and case studies shared in the book illustrate the huge impact that outsourcing can have on your business growth. Challenges like high operational costs, inventory management issues, and extended lead times, can all be solved through strategic outsourcing. This freedom from CAPEX, OPEX & daily operational headaches will free up your time and resources to build your brand and achieve remarkable growth and market presence.

Ultimately, the choice to outsource manufacturing is a strategic decision that can redefine your business journey.

It offers a pathway to efficiency, innovation, and market expansion, setting the stage for sustained success and profitability.

As you move forward, consider how outsourcing can be a catalyst for your growth, enabling you to seize opportunities, overcome obstacles, and achieve exceptional results.

Thank you for embarking on this journey with us. I look forward to further supporting you through the intricacies of outsourcing and helping you unlock its full potential. If you have any further questions on this or would love to go deeper. I'd be delighted to partner with you.

You can reach out to us at the number or e-mail id given below and my team will set up the next steps for a 1-2-1 session with me.

011-49004900

keshaavbhatia@grkcgroup.com

Give e-mail or phone number or appointment link or QR code